WORLD CULTURES

Living on the
Ganges River

Louise and Richard Spilsbury

Raintree

Chicago, Illinois

© 2008 Raintree
Published by Raintree,
a division of Reed Elsevier Inc.
Chicago, Illinois

Customer Service 888–454–2279

Visit our website at www.heinemannraintree.com

Designed by Richard Parker and Manhattan Design
Printed and bound in China by SCPC

12 11 10 09 08
10 9 8 7 6 5 4 3 2 1

Library of Congress Cataloging-in-Publication Data
Spilsbury, Louise and Richard.
Living on the Ganges River
p. cm. -- (World cultures)
Includes bibliographical references and index.
ISBN-13: 978-1-4109-2820-7 (library binding–hardcover)
ISBN-10: 1-4109-2820-9 (library binding–hardcover)
ISBN-13: 978-1-4109-2829-0 (pbk.)
ISBN-10: 1-4109-2829-2 (pbk.)
1. Varanasi (Uttar Pradesh, India)--Social life and
customs--Juvenile literature. 2. Ganges River (India and
Bangladesh)--Social life and customs--Juvenile literature.
3. Hindus--India--Varanasi (Uttar Pradesh)--Social life
and customs--Juvenile literature. I. Spilsbury, Richard,
1963- II. Title.
DS486.B4S65 2007
954'.2--dc22
                              2006037162

Acknowledgments
The publishers would like to thank the following for
permission to reproduce photographs: Alamy Images pp.
7 (Jon Arnold Images), **29** (Neil McAllister), **28** (Simon
Reddy); Circa Religion Photo Library/ Bip Mistry p. **8**;
Corbis pp. **12** (Lindsay Hebberd), **25** (Manjunath Kiran/
EPA); Eye Ubiquitous/Hutchison pp. **15**, **18**; Gamma/
Nusca Antonello p. **20**; Getty Images pp. **10** (Reportage/
Tom Stoddart), **24** (The Images Bank/ Chris Cheadle);
Harcourt Education Ltd/ Tudor Photography pp. **26**, **27**
(top and bottom); Lonely Planet Images/ Richard I'Anson
pp. **5**, **19**; Masterfile/ David Zimmerman p. **4**; OnAsia/
Alf Berg p. **11**; Rex Features pp. **9** (Patrick Frilet), **13**
(Upperhall Ltd/ Robert Harding); Robert Harding Picture
Library pp. **17** (Bruno Morandi), **22** (David Beatty), **14**
(Jeremy Bright), **23** (John Wilson), **16** (R H Productions),
21 (Tony Waltham).

Illustrations by International Mapping.

Cover photograph of pilgrims on the Ganges River,
Varanasi, India, reproduced with permission of Photo
Library/ Index Stock Imagery.

Every effort has been made to contact copyright holders
of any material reproduced in this book. Any omissions
will be rectified in subsequent printings if notice is given
to the publishers.

Contents

Some words are printed in bold, **like this**. You can find out what they mean on page 31.

Living Along the Ganges River

The Ganges River flows mainly through India, in Asia (see map on page 6). The river is special to the people of India. Millions of people live along its banks.

River of life

People have lived by the Ganges for thousands of years. They use its water for drinking, washing, cooking, and watering farmland. The river starts in the mountains and carries **sediment** as it flows. Sediment is soil and sand. Sediment makes land **fertile**. The land is good for growing crops.

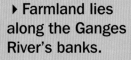
▸ Farmland lies along the Ganges River's banks.

Hindus and the Ganges

The Ganges is a **holy** river. Many Indian people are **Hindus**. They believe the Ganges came from heaven. The Ganges flows through the city of Varanasi in north India. Varanasi is a holy city. Hindus believe there is a path to heaven at this part of the Ganges.

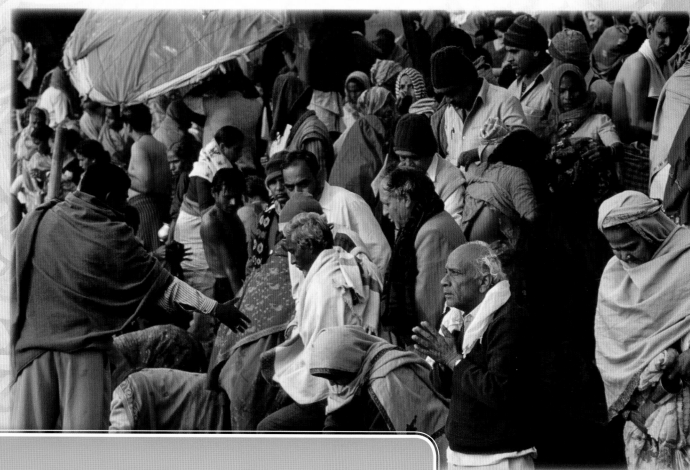

▲ Hindus from all over India come to Varanasi to worship by the river here.

A MAJOR WORLD RELIGION

Over 75 percent of the people in India are Hindus. Hindus live in many other parts of the world. Every Hindu hopes to visit Varanasi at least once in his or her lifetime. Over one million **pilgrims**, or visitors, come to Varanasi every year.

A River Region

The city of Varanasi is on the banks of the Ganges River. It is halfway along the river.

Along the river

The Ganges River is the longest river in India. It is about 1,500 miles (2,500 kilometers) long. Its **source**, or starting point, is in the mountains. On steep mountain slopes, the river moves quickly. Few people live here. In the middle parts, the river flows over flat land. Here, it is quite wide and moves steadily. Many people live in this area. The lowest part of the Ganges River is in Bangladesh. This is where it joins the sea.

▶ Can you find Varanasi on this map?

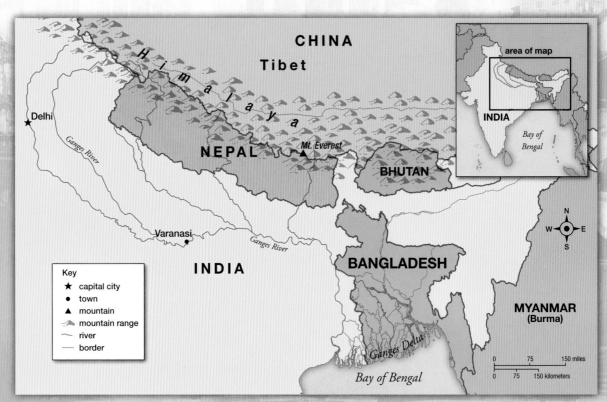

▲ The monsoon rains swell the Ganges River. The floodwater can fill city streets.

Heat and monsoon

In India it is warm all year, except in the highest mountains. There are wet and dry seasons. The wet season is called the **monsoon**. Winds bring heavy rain and it rains heavily almost every day. Sometimes it rains so much the Ganges River spills over its banks. It floods the land around it.

GANGES DOLPHIN

Ganges river dolphins live in the river. They are blind. They hunt for fish using **echolocation**. The dolphin sends out high-pitched squeaks and listens to the echoes to locate fish!

Temples and Homes

Varanasi has many **temples**. Some temples are huge. They tower over the Ganges and have steps down to the river. Other temples are small and simple. Many of the streets and alleys in Varanasi are narrow. They were built before there were cars.

▲ A Hindu boy prays at a shrine in his home.

Inside a Hindu house

Houses in Varanasi often have open yards inside. Rooms are arranged around the yards. The rooms are simple. They have concrete or wooden floors to keep them cool. You might not find a refrigerator or washing machine, but there is often a small television. There is always a **shrine**, where families pray.

A shrine has pictures or statues of gods or goddesses. There is a holder for burning **incense**. Incense is a kind of perfume. There are bowls for **offerings** to the gods. They contain food or flowers. A shrine can be on a windowsill, in a corner of a room, or even inside a cupboard.

▶ Many doorways have carvings of the elephant god, Ganesh. This is to bring good luck.

OLD PEOPLE'S HOMES

Hindus believe that dying in Varanasi means they will go straight to heaven. Many of the buildings here are old people's homes.

In a Hindu Community

The **Hindu community** in Varanasi centers on the Ganges. A Hindu's job is often decided by the person's position in Indian society.

Down at the ghats

The **ghats** are the city's wide stone steps that lead down to the Ganges River. People visit the steps from early morning until nighttime. Most people come to bathe in the river. They believe it cleanses them of their **sins**. Other people come to play sports, meet friends, or rest. Some people bring umbrellas to shade them from the Sun. Boatmen use the steps to reach their boats.

▼ There are about 100 ghats in Varanasi. They stretch for about 4 miles (more than 6 kilometers) along the river!

▲ Hindu children born into a family from the farming caste usually become farmers themselves.

Castes

Traditionally, every Hindu is born into a **caste**. There are five castes, or groups. A caste can affect the job a person does and how much respect he or she gets from people. The *Dalit* people are in the lowest caste. They often have to beg or do jobs no one else wants to do. *Dalit* people may live on the streets of Varanasi. They clear litter and waste left by **pilgrims**. They also take care of the remains of dead bodies. Bodies are **cremated** (burned) in ceremonies on funeral ghats.

11

Daily Life

In many **Hindu** families, children, parents, grandparents, and even aunts and uncles all live together. They often work together as well.

Work

Many people in Varanasi work in tourism. They run guesthouses for visitors. Some work in restaurants or in food stands. Others take tourists on trips or are farmers. The Ganges provides a lot of work. Fishermen catch fish from the Ganges. Other boatmen use rowboats to move along the river. Many of the metal workers in the city make pots for carrying water from the river. Builders use sand from the riverbanks for building.

▲ Fishermen sort out the fish they have caught from the Ganges River.

▲ Being the driver of a cycle rickshaw can be very hard work.

Getting around

Cars are used on the main streets. The old part of the city is very narrow. People walk or cycle in the narrow parts. Sometimes they travel by cycle rickshaw. A cycle rickshaw is a bicycle-taxi. Visitors usually arrive in the city by train. Many take boat trips along the Ganges to see the busy **ghats**.

COWS IN THE STREET

Drivers have to watch out for more than just people on the city streets. Cows are sacred (**holy**) to the Hindu **community**. They are allowed to wander freely around the city.

Food and Mealtimes

Family meals at home are usually made from fresh ingredients. People buy the ingredients each day. Before eating a meal, the family says a prayer.

▲ The smells of freshly fried food are very tempting.

Types of foods

Most **Hindus** are **vegetarians**, although some do eat fish and meat. Hindus do not eat beef. Beef comes from a cow. Cows are sacred animals to Hindus. Most main meals are made with rice and lentils. Fresh vegetables are grown locally. Chutneys are thick sauces made from fruit, such as mangoes and bananas. Yogurt is made from cow's milk and is very popular.

Street food

Food stands sell food to workers and tourists. There are syrupy desserts and savory snacks, including *samosas* and *kachodi*. *Samosas* are triangular pastry shells filled with spicy vegetables. *Kachodi* are crispy wheat puffs stuffed with potato, peas, and lentils. These snacks are often sold wrapped in banana leaves. The leaves are from trees nearby.

◀ Everyone washes their hands before eating. They do not use knives, forks, and spoons. Most people eat using their right hand.

COOL DRINK

A good drink to have to cool down on a hot day is *thandi*. *Thandi* is made with cold yogurt, almonds, and spices.

Clothing and Decoration

Hindu men wear suits, jeans, or a *dhoti*. A *dhoti* is a cotton cloth wrapped around the waist. It is a good way to keep cool. Women mostly wear *saris* or *salwar kameez*. *Saris* are long, colorful cloths wound around the body and worn over a simple top. The *salwar kameez* are baggy pants. They are worn under a long shirt.

◀ Hindu women tend to wear traditional clothes, while most Hindu men wear cotton shirts and pants.

Varanasi silk

Expensive *saris* are made from Varanasi silk. This silk is made on **silkworm** farms in the area. In the past, silk traders transported silk along the Ganges to sell in other places. They grew rich and built the grand **temples** in the city.

Body decorations

Women wear bangles, necklaces, earrings, and nose rings. These often have special meanings. A woman wears bangles if she is married. Her bangles are removed if her husband dies. Married women also wear a *bindi*. A *bindi* is a colored spot on the forehead. At parties, jasmine and marigold flowers are often placed around a guest's neck.

▲ These are **henna** hand patterns. Some patterns are said to keep away bad luck.

BATHING SUITS

Women wear their *saris* when they bathe in the Ganges. Men wear a *gamcha* to bathe. A *gamcha* is a thin cotton towel.

School

For many children in Varanasi, the school day starts with some stretching exercises. These happen outdoors to wake everybody up. In summer it can be too hot for this. They may have songs and a prayer indoors instead.

Schooltime

School starts at 8:30 a.m. Children take reading, writing, and math classes. The classes are given in the **Hindi** language. At lunchtime many children receive a free lunch. This is usually a hot meal of lentils and rice. Some schools have a uniform.

◄ These school children in Varanasi are lined up to do their morning exercises.

▸ This child should be in school. Instead, she is working. She is selling little baskets for people to send **offerings** on the Ganges River.

Poverty

Some children in Varanasi are from very poor families. These children do not go to school. Families do not have to pay to send children to school, but they must pay for the uniform, books, and supplies. Some families cannot afford to do this. Some families also need the money their children can earn from working.

RIVER LESSONS

Today, school children learn how **polluted**, or dirty, the Ganges River has become. It is best not to drink its water.

Leisure Time

The people of Varanasi spend their free time in different ways. Some children in Varanasi play computer games. They also play games of chase and hide-and-seek. Boys play **cricket** or soccer on flat areas alongside the river. They swim in its water as well. Men sit cross-legged on the ground playing chess.

Children play simple games, such as *chukki*, with things they find. They draw a circle in the dusty road. Then, they take turns aiming stones at the circle. They try to knock each other's stones out of the circle.

▸ Barefoot young boys play soccer.

Going to the movies

Families in Varanasi like going to the movies. Most Indian movies are not based on real life. People work hard to earn money, so the movies they like to see show a fantasy world. People can escape into the movies, away from their problems. Indian movies are usually colorful and noisy. They have songs, dances, comedy, and thrills!

▶ Movie theaters often have the soundtracks to movies blaring into the street. This is to tempt people inside.

OLD AND NEW

The city of Varanasi is an exciting mix of old and new. There are ancient stone **temples** and figures decorated with fresh flowers. Alongside these are huge billboards advertising brand new movies in clashing colors.

Music and Drama

Legend says that the god Shiva made his home on Earth in Varanasi. Shiva is the god of dance and music in the **Hindu** religion.

Indian instruments

Some people come to Varanasi to learn, hear, or buy traditional Indian instruments. These instruments are made locally. The *sitar* is a long, stringed instrument with a rounded, wooden body. The *tabla* is a pair of hand drums made from wood, metal, or clay. These instruments are often played together at concerts or in **temples**.

◄ Flutes are another popular Hindu instrument. These musicians are playing at a spring festival.

THE POWER OF SONG

Singing is important in Indian culture. It is a feature of temple life. You can often hear chanting or singing in the streets. Many people come to Varanasi to learn to sing traditional songs and play traditional Indian instruments.

◀ Children dress up in colorful costumes and makeup to take part in *Ram Leela*.

Acting out legends

Most Hindus learn and enjoy stories from the **holy** book *Ramayana*. Each year special stages are built across Varanasi for a festival called the *Ram Leela*. During the *Ram Leela*, people dance. They act out characters from the *Ramayana*, such as the monkey god, Hanuman. The story unfolds on different stages. Thousands of people move around the city to see the whole story.

Festivals

There is a traditional saying, "Every day is a great festival in Varanasi." It is true! There are more festivals in the **Hindu** calendar than days in the year!

Ganga puja

Ganga puja is a huge festival in June. It celebrates the arrival of the Ganges River on Earth. Thousands of people come to bathe in the Ganges on this day. Those people who cannot come to the river try to have some Ganges water in their homes at this time.

▶ During *Ganga puja*, Hindus float candles out onto the river.

▲ *Holi* is wild, noisy, and fun.

Holi

The festival of *Holi* happens in March. The fields are full of crops. The festival is a celebration of spring. People light bonfires, beat hand drums, and sing. The highlight for most people is the chance to throw brightly colored paint over each other and at passersby.

COLORS OF HOLI

The colors thrown at *Holi* have different meanings: red represents purity, green means life, blue **symbolizes** calmness, and yellow means religious feelings.

Tie-Dye a T-shirt

Holi is known as the festival of color. Tie-dye a T-shirt or other piece of cloth to create your own riot of color!

To tie-dye a T-shirt, you will need:
- a white T-shirt (ideally cotton)
- some pebbles, rubber bands, and rubber gloves
- a bowl with water and some fabric dye.

Step 1

Place a pebble onto the T-shirt and wrap it in the fabric with a rubber band. Fix on two or three more pebbles.

Step 2

Put on the gloves and follow the instructions on the dye package. Ask an adult to help. Put the colored fabric dye in water in the bowl. Soak your T-shirt for as long as it says on the package.

Step 3

Wear your gloves to take out the T-shirt. Remove the rubber bands and pebbles. Rinse it and then dry it. Now, it is ready to wear!

NATURAL DYE

Many people in India use natural dyes. They use beet juice or onion skin to color fabric. If you are feeling adventurous, you could try this instead. But get an adult to help you—it can be very messy.

Varanasi and the Ganges

The city of Varanasi was created because of its location on the Ganges. The river is badly **polluted** now, but it is still important to the city.

City of light

When Varanasi was built around 3,000 years ago, it was called *Kashi*. *Kashi* means the "city of light." The Ganges flows south, but at Varanasi it bends north. For **Hindus** this change of direction **symbolizes** life. Hindus built Varanasi on the west banks of the river. The **ghats** face the rising Sun. People pray here early in the day.

▶ Saddhus are Hindu holy men. Many Saddhus come to Varanasi to worship the Ganges.

River rituals

Bathing in the river is an important Hindu **ritual**. Another ancient ritual happens on the funeral ghats. These are places for **cremating** (burning) dead bodies. Families float the ashes of their loved ones in the Ganges. Hindus believe the **holy** water takes them to heaven.

The Ganges today

Today, the Ganges is very polluted. People fear it is not healthy to perform rituals in its waters. The pollution comes from factories. They release waste into the water. Pollution also comes from sewage. Sewage is waste from toilets and drains. Sometimes dead bodies float in the sacred water. They are placed there when a family cannot afford a cremation ceremony.

▲ In Varanasi it is much safer to get your water from a faucet than to drink the river water.

Find Out for Yourself

Books to read

Bowden, Rob. *The Ganges* (*A River Journey* series). Chicago: Raintree, 2004.

Chambers, Catherine, and N. Lapthorn. *Rivers* (*Mapping Earthforms* series). Chicago: Heinemann Library, 2007.

Parker, Victoria. *The Ganges* (*Holy Places* series). Chicago: Raintree, 2003.

Wood, Angela. *Hindu Mandir.* (*Places of Worship* series). Milwaukee: Gareth Stevens, 2000.

Websites

www.uri.org/kids/world_hind.htm
For a guide to Hinduism, look at this website.

www.hindunet.org/day_as_hindu/
Find out what it would be like to spend a day as a Hindu.

www.timeforkids.com/TFK/specials/goplaces/0,12405,214513,00.html
Learn more about India at this site, including sights to see, historical facts, and helpful words and phrases.

Glossary

bindi small, colored dot worn in the middle of a married woman's forehead

caste particular group or class of people in a country

community group of people who either live in a particular local area or share something important, such as following the same religion

cremate burn a dead body as part of a funeral ceremony

cricket sport in which two teams compete on a large field using a ball and bat

echolocation system used by some animals to find their way in the dark. Bats, for example, give out high-pitched squeaks and then use the echoes to find their way around.

fertile ground that is good for growing healthy plants in

ghat wide stone step that connects Varanasi city to the Ganges River

henna plant dye used to color hair and to decorate hands and feet

Hindi official language of India

Hindu person who follows the Hindu religion

holy something that is special because of its connection with god

incense perfumed substance that releases its scent when burned

monsoon winds that bring heavy rain to an area for a season

offering gift to gods and goddesses

pilgrim person who travels to a place that is sacred or special to his or her religion

polluted when water, air, or land is damaged or made dirty

ritual action that people do in a particular way as part of a religious ceremony

sediment grains of sand and soil that sink in water

shrine holy or sacred place dedicated to a certain god, goddess, or other religious figure

silkworm caterpillar of the Asian silkworm moth that produces threads of silk

sin when somebody does something that is against his or her god's wishes or teachings

source beginning of a river. Many rivers have their source on a hill or a mountain.

symbolize when something stands in for something else. For example, red often symbolizes danger.

temple place where people go to worship their god

vegetarian person who does not eat meat

Index